Sacred Geometry
FOR THE SOUL

ANN CHATFIELD

A Wood Dragon Book

Sacred Geometry
FOR THE SOUL

VOLUME I

Written and Illustrated by

*The Masters, Angels, Teachers, Loved Ones
and Guides
of
Human Ann Chatfield*

A Wood Dragon Book

Sacred Geometry for the Soul - Volume I
Copyright 2022 Ann Chatfield

All rights reserved. This book or any portion thereof may not be reproduced in part or in whole without the express written permission of the author or publisher except for the use of brief quotations in a critical review.

Cover design: Callum Jagger
Author photo by: Milton Taylor - Image Photography
Interior design: Christine Lee
The poem "Desiderata" by Max Ehrmann (public domain)

Published by:
Wood Dragon Books
Post Office Box 429
Mossbank, Saskatchewan, Canada S0H3G0
www.wooddragonbooks.com

Available in hardcover, paperback, and eBook
ISBN: Paperback 978-1-990863-06-6
ISBN: Hardcover 978-1-990863-07-3
ISBN: eBook 978-1-990863-10-3

Author contact information:
Email: ann@powerportalsolutions.com
Website: www.powerportalsolutions.com

Dedication

This book is dedicated to my ancestors who have given me the gift of life and of family. I am so grateful and I love you.

To my husband—for being my greatest love on this journey and one of my greatest teachers. Thank you for allowing me the space to listen to my own soul, my intuition and to my guides; I know at times this has not been an easy road. I love you.

To my children—for choosing me as your mother in this life. I have learned so much from each of you—from experiencing the miracle of holding you in my arms for the first time to letting you go on to create lives of your own. I have enjoyed watching you pick your treasured life partners and grow your own families. I love you and those you have chosen to share your life with.

To my grandchildren—you continue to inspire me to love deeper, to play and have more joy on my journey. I love you.

I pray that all of you and all who read this book find joy and purpose in this life and evolve to your highest potential. I love you.

Table of Contents

INTRODUCTION AND WELCOME ... 1

PART I

MY STORY ... 5
THE AKASHIC RECORDS ... 10
POWER PORTAL MANDALAS ... 13
SACRED GEOMETRY AND SYMBOLS ... 22
THE ENERGY OF COLORS AND THEIR MEANINGS ... 30
THE SEVEN BASIC CHAKRAS IN SACRED GEOMETRY ... 34
WHAT IS A MANDALA? ... 37
USING POWER PORTAL MANDALAS FOR MEDITATION ... 40

PART II

HEALING ... 46
EXPANDED POTENTIAL ... 48
ROOT CHAKRA ... 50
SACRAL CHAKRA ... 52
SOLAR PLEXUS CHAKRA ... 54
HEART CHAKRA ... 56
THROAT CHAKRA ... 58
THIRD EYE CHAKRA ... 60
CROWN CHAKRA ... 62
HIGHEST POTENTIAL ... 64
FEMALE MALE BALANCE ... 66
DNA ENHANCEMENT ... 68
ANCESTRAL PAST ... 70
BACK TO "OM" ... 72
STAND TALL ... 74
PINEAL GLAND EXPANSION ... 76
YOU ARE AMAZING ... 78
DEEP WITHIN ... 80

LIFE IS PURE BLISS	82	EXPECT GOOD THINGS	130
FEEL IT, HEAL IT, AND LET IT GO	84	BUILD BRIDGES	132
UNWIND, PLAY AND GROW	86	REACH OUT	134
YOU ARE PERFECT	88	CHOICE	136
INTUITIVE PUSH	90	MOVE ON	138
REJUVENATION	92	INSIDE OUTSIDE	140
FORGIVE YOURSELF	94	WATER	142
CELEBRATE YOUR WINS	96	CHOOSE & ENJOY THE JOURNEY	144
EXUBERANCE	98	RENEWAL/BIRTH	146
OUT OF THE BLUE	100	ANCHORED IN LOVE	148
BLOOM	102	NORTHERN LIGHTS	150
LET IT GO	104	LEGIONS OF ANGELS	152
YOU ARE LOVED	106	BALANCE AND HARMONY	154
FLOURISH	108	EYE ON THE EARTH	156
BOUNDARIES FOR GROWTH	110	SPOT ON	158
ACCEPTANCE	112	ANGELS AMONG US	160
SEE CLEARLY	114	GRATITUDE STARTS WITHIN	162
TO INFINITY AND BEYOND	116	LOVE WHERE YOU LIVE	164
CENTER SUN	118	PEACEFUL LIFE	166
DIVINE LOVE	120	LISTEN TO THE SPIRIT OF THE EARTH	168
THRIVE	122	RAINBOW WARRIOR	170
OFF KILTER	124		
TURN AROUND	126		
ASK FOR HELP	128		

PART III

CONCLUSION	173
ACKNOWLEDGEMENTS	177
ABOUT THE AUTHOR	181
WORKING WITH ANN	183

Introduction and Welcome

*"I have no words to describe how the first time felt,
it was beyond any magic that I could imagine.
How could this be happening?
The message, the innocence, the divine perfection,
the beauty…
With the creation of each new addition,
I wondered…
Could I feel more love? More than before?
And once again, I was expanded by this love."*

I channeled and created this book of mandalas because I believe we are all in this life to experience and magnify divine love in each and every moment.

It is not by chance you are reading this book.
You are in the right place!
Know that you are divinely perfect.
You are part of a bigger plan.
You are okay.
Right here…right now.
Breathe…Breathe…Breathe…

How do I know this and why do I write these words? Because I have felt and seen the energy of love all my life. I just did not know how to explain it. I studied traditional religion while participating in the Catholic, Anglican, and United churches. I studied the Wheel of Life, Buddhism and some new age systems. I studied Nature, Educational Kinesiology, Essential Oils, Crystals, Reiki, Yuen, Oneness Blessing, Access Bars, and Akashic Record Reading and more—looking for answers about why we are here and how we can live our best life. In each of these religions, holistic healing modalities and practices, I searched for ways to help myself become a better human, to understand the complexities of who I was, and for ways of healing both myself and of helping others through the rough spots in life. I always thought that there was support to move through the challenges life brings, and that each day we were made to be better than the day before. None of these religious practices or individual modalities were big enough to support my perception of God, healing, and how I thought the Universe responded to my needs.

I have worked with individuals and groups from across North America to address and resolve life issues, strengthen connection to spirit, and provide clarity about their life purpose. Working with living human beings and crossed-over souls has tested and solidified my beliefs on many levels. I have worked with energy for the last three decades and have finally figured out that sharing this knowledge with you is indeed a great part of my purpose.

I love the concept that as we raise our own energy and keep it balanced and aligned, we attract a vibrational match to our own energy, and all that is not a vibrational match simply is not attracted to us. This does not mean that life is always smooth and rosy, it simply means that life has better meaning and flow, enabling us to understand and learn more.

While I was intently asking about my purpose in my own Akashic Records, I continuously was shown the word *mandala*, heard the word *mandala*, and told to create a simple modality to help others. I was told to share the mandalas with the world. Fulfilling this message has been a continuing journey of change, learning about the Akashic records, about sacred geometry, about mandalas, and about my life path.

Through my research and working with mandalas, I have learned that all of us are a part of each other, of the earth, and of the systems within our Universe. We are intricately connected to each other in the unlimited and ever-abundant response system of the Universe. Connected to the good, the bad and the ugly, we are here to experience life on every level and to expand love.

Not one of us is better or worse than another. There is no hierarchy. We are who we are. Each of us is unique to our own journey. The more we can learn about our purpose and who we are, the more we can expand the love that we are meant to be and tap into the gifts we bring to the world. It is beneficial to all of us to see everyone succeed and fulfill their purpose in this life, as we are all connected throughout the Universe. It truly is an *"All for one and one for all"* life!

Spending time with these mandalas will help you see your own divine magnificence and learn to reach your highest potential in every moment. It is in living each day to the fullest that we create a life of love and purpose. A life where we can openly evolve and share our gifts with the world. We can change the world by making an effort to reach our own highest potential each day and by expanding our love. The world needs us now!

My Story

I was born on a farm in northeast Saskatchewan, the eighth of nine children. I could see energy from a very early age. When I was about three, I could see rainbow auras around the frogs swimming in our pond. In my farmyard, I could see the daisies and willows glowing with light and energy. I thought it was normal, that everyone could see these energy fields.

As a child, my favorite thing to do was to spend time outdoors—and as a result, I developed a very strong connection to nature. This was where I was first exposed to sacred geometry; witnessing many natural forms of sacred geometry in the flowers, pinecones and in the patterns on snowflakes.

I often played with my siblings in the outdoor playhouse that was built in an old truck box. Sometimes, I laid on top of the little oil shed for hours watching the sky and the birds. My favorite place to sit was beside our little farm pond on a huge rock, watching the frogs croak, the tadpoles develop, the ducks swim, and enjoying the sun with our dog Tiny. Occasionally, I would get to play with my friends that lived a mile or two down the road. We would play saving the world—imagining the chickens, cats, pigs, and chipmunks were all there to help.

Except for Saturday night bath time and going to Church on Sunday, my life as a child was very free and unstructured. Until I was sent away to school at a convent.

My parents always did what they thought was best for their children; they wanted us to get a good education, speak both French and English well, and have a good religious upbringing. Therefore, when I was six years old, my parents sent me to the convent with my older siblings. The students stayed there for months at a time without going home. There were rules everywhere and I was traumatized and very homesick.

The nuns and other students spoke French, which I found confusing. I was punished for crawling into my older sisters' beds and made to stay up all night and pray to be a good girl. I shut down most of my own energy and within six months of being placed in the convent, my body became ill and feverish. I do not remember what was wrong with me, but I do remember my parents coming to the hospital and being very concerned over my high fever.

After my parents left, I started to cry. The little Statue of Mother Mary in the alcove of my room talked to me and comforted me. Each time I was alone or scared during my hospital stay, she comforted me. She taught me that I was loved unconditionally by something bigger than my parents and my family; she encouraged and convinced me that there was a purpose here for me.

She has appeared to bring me comfort and guidance many times throughout my life and her energy resides not only in my soul, but in the *Mother Mary Queen of Angels* mandala that sits above my desk. I am very grateful for this connection and ongoing support.

I only remained at the convent for my Grade One year, but I often would talk to Mother Mary when I needed her. I kept my conversations with her to myself—I was old enough to know I would be made fun of or punished for sharing this information.

Just like I believed that others could see auras surrounding frogs, I thought everyone had this connection with Mother Mary, but just never talked about it. I went through school holding back the things I saw and felt, just as I thought everyone else went about their days hiding the things they saw and felt. I thought knowing this connection and keeping it to yourself was part of what was required, what made us good, what made us lovable, and what God wanted from us. I wanted to be good and do my best in every situation, and I wanted people to be happy.

As I grew, I continued to feel these connections to energy, to God, to Mother Mary, and to nature. At 13, I felt a connection that was bigger than I understood. In a pool hall in Saskatchewan, when I first placed my eyes on my life partner, my best teacher and the love of my life, I knew I could not hide the feelings of connection that pulled us together.

Although our life together has not always been perfect or easy, our love for each other has grown. We have been together for nearly 50 years; we have been blessed with four wonderful children, their four fabulous partners and ten very loved grandchildren. I am so grateful they picked me to share their lives with. Of all the things I have experienced in this life, without a doubt, being a wife, mother, mother-in-law, and grandmother are among the most cherished and are the experiences that continue to accelerate my ability to love beyond what I think is possible.

I have had several careers and multiple jobs, but nothing ever satisfied my desire to serve and help make the world a better place. I often felt unfulfilled. I knew there was "something" I wanted to do in this life. I had a gift to share with the world, but what was it? I spent years trying to answer the questions "Why am I here? What is my purpose? What does this all mean?" I now know the answers to some of these questions and know what my gift is. I am excited to share it with you through illustration and explanation of these channeled Power Portal mandalas. I know you are all part of my soul family and I hope the mandalas help you to find peace in who you are and to reach the highest potential on your journey.

The Akashic Records

Before we explore the mandalas, it is useful to understand what the Akashic Records are, and how they are accessed.

Edgar Cayce, the psychic medium described them as "The Book of Life." They can be equated to the Universe's super-computer system that acts as the central storehouse of all information for every individual who has ever lived upon the earth. More than just a reservoir of events, these records contain every deed, word, feeling, thought, and intent that has ever occurred at any time in the history of the world. The Akashic Records are interactive in that they have a tremendous influence upon our everyday lives, our relationships, our feelings and belief systems, and the potential realities we draw toward us. They contain the entire history of every soul since the dawn of Creation and can be accessed to reveal the clear truth that provides the freedom to choose our paths with grace in all things.

The Akashic Records can be understood as the energetic imprint of all experiences of all lifetimes and in all realities. They are a storage system from the spiritual world where we can access any information from the human consciousness from the past, the present and the future. It is a huge library, run by spiritual teachers, ancestors and guides. It is open to provide guidance and support. It is an energy source for all to use. The energy that makes up the Akashic Records is a very high frequency of energy comparable to the frequency of love—an unconditional love that permeates and creates everything and everyone in our Universe.

The Akashic Records are like the DNA of the Universe. They contain a collection of everything that has occurred in the past, create the virtual reality of the present, and hold information regarding the possibilities for the future. Every individual soul has its own, unique Akashic Record. These records connect us to our highest potential, to our soul families and to one another through our massive interactive universal system.

Consider the flashes of intuition and knowing hunches that occur every day. These are glimpses into the divine wisdom contained in the Akashic Records. Everyone can access information from the Akashic Records, either with the help of an intuitive coach or by themselves. With training, individuals can learn to know when they are in their records and how to find direction when they are seeking guidance.

My job as an intuitive coach is to access and work in these records and to do a search for the *Highest Potential* of an individual's soul to help the individual get the answers they seek about their life, abundance, relationships, career, and purpose. Accessing Akashic records is my favorite modality when I work with others because it is an interactive process where I provide needed information to help boost the individual on their life path and to find more joy in their journey.

It was through meditation in my own Akashic records that I began to create the mandalas. Over time, I realized that each mandala has a different message and is here to help us move forward with more grace and ease.

Power Portal Mandalas

My career as an HR manager had come to an end in 2012, due to a layoff. I was living with chronic pain in my knees and feet. I was not sure that I wanted to go back to work, or that I could go back to work. I spent part of 2013 in Florida helping my sister who was dying of cancer. After my sister passed away, I was exhausted on all levels. Although Mother Mary was with me through it all, I was mad at God for taking my sister, and I was still looking for answers.

I became a new practitioner of the Akashic Records in 2016, and was very focused on finding out my purpose in this life and on healing my own self.

It was during this time of rebuilding my body and focusing on my future, that I kept seeing the word *"mandala"* in my Akashic records. I did not really know what a mandala was, so I initially ignored these messages, my human brain dismissing them as not important. When the messages continued to come, I booked sessions with other practitioners to have them ask about my purpose. When one told me that I was painting round things, like wheels, I was a little surprised; but when the second one told me that I was the creator of a new system of communication and healing, I was both terrified and excited. I still did not understand how all of this was connected to the word *mandala* or that the use of mandalas was the system they were referring to.

For months, my brain went through all the self-help healing techniques I had learned, trying to find my new system or modality. As I continued to look for this new way to help myself and others live their best lives, I did not make the connection between the urging to create mandalas and the development of a new, simple and easy-to-use system for self-healing and support.

Only after breaking my thumb on my right hand during a backwoods quad riding expedition—and having surgery to repair it—did I finally start down the mandala road. My physiotherapist told me to write, doodle or paint for an hour a day to bring back dexterity and strength in my thumb. I decided to achieve two goals at once: strengthening my thumb and making this mandala that kept showing up in my records.

I watched videos on making mandalas and read articles about what they were and how to make one. I settled in on the dot painting technique as it seemed the most aligned with my talents and abilities.

For four afternoons, a couple of hours each day, I painted tiny acrylic dots on a canvas with the end of my paint brush handle. Suddenly, I felt like making a freehand fresh swoop—not at all in line with the mandala I was trying to make. It looked bad, very bad. I got the brainwave that if I took the mandala over to the sink, I could wash off the wet acrylic paint and salvage the dot filled center that had taken approximately six hours to create. This made perfect sense as the center had been dry on the canvas for at least a day.

After acrylic paint has dried on a canvas for a day it does not usually wash out. However, when I took the mandala to the sink, absolutely *all* the paint washed off with the first spray … all the dots … all my work.

I was mad at myself for washing away my work—but I was madder that I had wasted time in making a stupid mandala, something I knew nothing about!

I said out loud, "Well, if you guys want me to make a mandala, you are going to have to give me step-by-step instructions. As you can see, I don't know what I am doing with this!"

I sat down in my chair with a glass of water, put ice on my sore thumb, turned on my meditation music, and opened my Akashic Records. It was then I started to hear step-by-step instructions from my guides.

The instructions were simple and basic. *Stay in the Akashic records and connect with the guides. Take a pencil and write words on the canvas. This is the first layer because words carry a form of energy all their own. Cover the canvas with acrylic paint, usually metallic to reflect the light, but not always. The backgrounds are made by picking up colors as directed and squirting or dripping them onto a canvas. They are not painted by putting paint on a palette and painting stroke by stroke. Once the background is dry, the mandala design will be sent in a clear image piece by piece, starting with the center and working outward.*

As I settled into the Akashic Records, the words on the canvas came quickly and were penciled in. Next, my hands were guided to a brush, a sponge, a rag and then moved the paint around the canvas. Most mandalas have only one coat of paint on the background, some up to three to get the result my guides seek. I get a clear message when each stage is complete. If the message is not clear, I ask what else is needed and direction is always there.

I made several mandalas during 2018 and 2019 while recovering from knee replacement surgery, but I still did not realize that the mandalas themselves were the simple self-help tool I was looking for! I have now grown to understand that each mandala has a different message. They hold healing light codes within the color and design of each mandala. These codes are activated upon sight and are updated by a team of guides on a continual basis as each new mandala is made. Over time, the collection of mandalas has become the new holistic, simple-to-use system or modality that I was looking for.

The canvas may dry a day or a month before the mandala design is channeled through to me from my guides. Each stroke is shown to me and created as directed from the guides in the Akashic realm. It is important to connect the lines from the center out and keep the connection going. This helps them move energy. While being created, special music is selected and played to also add to their energy. The mandalas are given a *Oneness Blessing* to connect them to *All That Is*, a Reiki treatment to balance and align their energy, and a *Mother Mary* blessing because she is a strong supporter of the mandalas and my purpose in this life. The mandala is often infused with sun and moon energies, connecting them to natural elements of our environment so they can provide a natural support to our lives. *All That Is* is a phrase that describes the "everything" that exists, the whole of creation, including you.

When it is time to make a mandala, it is time. I have made mandalas through the night and at all times of the day. There is no point in trying to do something else, as it will not go well until the energy of the mandala is put on the canvas.

I follow the instructions I am given from my guides, starting each mandala at the center. Although I use a basic geometry set for some parts, lids from jars, bowls, bottle caps, wooden and plastic shapes are traced to create the shape and look that is needed. The mandalas are organically drawn while I am in a state of meditation. When they are done, they are done. Sometimes it takes just one sitting to finish a mandala, sometimes it takes two or three sittings to have the message complete. Once complete, they are given a name.

In 2020, I realized that each mandala has its own message. It was then that I began to use them with groups and individual clients to move energy and deliver their own unique message. The results were amazing; people shifted before my eyes simply by resting their gaze on a mandala for a couple of minutes.

In late November of 2021, I still could not find the modality or system I had been seeking. I needed some outside clarification. I attended a session with Intuitive Channeler Bonnie Bogner who called in the Galactic Council of Light, an intergalactic organization that gives spiritual guidance. During this call, I was told to make the mandalas into a book and to use them for the good of our planet right now. I debated if this was the right path for me and if I wanted to be the person to put this out into our world. I was not sure I could be open about all the things I see and feel. I was not prepared to take this leap.

Once again, the Universe proved it had other plans for me.

I have come to realize that I don't always listen very well to my guides. Unfortunately, when we do not listen to our own soul, when we are not in touch with our chosen path, our human bodies get denser and attract more negative energies. In December of 2021, I was diagnosed with thyroid cancer. This stopped me in my tracks.

I thought, *What if this is the beginning of the end? What if it has spread? What about my family, my grandkids, my life? Have I done everything I can in this lifetime to make the world a better place? Do the people I love know how much I love them?*

And then it hit me. *What about the gift of the mandalas…what if their energy stops in my office? What if they never inspire others to grow? What if the love they bring to the world dies if I do?*

The thyroid is located in the throat. It is the energy center from which we speak our truth. It is where my voice is located. The voice that I have hidden, the voice that was often silenced because of fear of being judged, fear of losing those I love, fear of being seen. With this book, I am letting go of those fears. It is time to be love-in-action with all I do and with those around me, to put my fears behind me, and to put the mandalas out into the world to reach their highest potential.

I am not a famous or great artist. I am not a sacred geometry specialist. I am me. I am prepared to listen to my guides and to share these mandalas with you.

The more time I spend in my Akashic records, the stronger my intuition becomes and the more I can understand the information that is presented. In the past, I tried putting this energy out in the world, but the time was not right. The guides have told me that the time is now, and the Council of Light has agreed—years of searching, researching, and of creating mandalas is making this path clear. This is the new modality/system that my guides were talking about! This is what I asked for, something easy, that anyone can benefit from, that does not require extensive weekend courses, does not have a lot of rules, and is available to all of mankind, no matter what age, language, or religious belief.

The Akashic guides refer to these mandalas as *Power Portals*, as they are meant to help move people through rough spots and lift the energy up to its highest frequency. They align and balance everything in a subtle simple way for people to help themselves through times of turmoil, without having to leave their home and seek out a practitioner. They are made to upgrade energy in anyone who sees them, even if for only a moment.

They recalibrate and harmonize our energy. They are here to help each of us get our true power back. They are indeed a *Power Portal* to our soul and to the new world that we are creating. Welcome to the experience of the *Power Portal Mandalas!* Each person will have their own experience and their own journey as we are all here for a different reason. Each of us has a purpose and gift to bring to the world.

Sacred Geometry and Symbols

In the mandalas I create, I use both *common* geometry symbols as well as *sacred* geometry symbols as determined by my guides. Further in this chapter, is a listing of the symbols used in this book. The listing is meant to be a guide, as what matters most is *your* interpretation of the Power Portal mandalas and *your* soul journey.

Sacred geometry is considered an ancient science that explores and explains the energy patterns that create and unify all things in our Universe and beyond. It is the binding element of our Universe and is literally the blueprint of human beings and of our world. It reveals the precise way that the energy of creation organizes itself to create matter.

If you look closely, you can see that every natural pattern of growth or movement comes back to one or more simple geometric shapes. Snowflakes, flowers, succulents, seashells, the stars, the galaxy we spiral within, the air we breathe—even the strands of our DNA—all life forms are created out of sacred geometric codes and numeric sequences.

From the beginning of time, humans have tried to draw and create ideas and concepts with the aim of passing their knowledge on to future generations. By using the simplest sacred geometry shapes that are found in nature such as the circle, the triangle and the square, many cultures in the world were able to deliver and preserve different messages. Although many of these sacred geometric shapes are used as religious symbols, the ones used in these mandalas are not linked to any specific religion and are meant to be open to your own interpretation and beliefs.

The power of sacred geometry and its beauty has been used by architects, musicians, artists, and philosophers from all around the world for many years. This is not something new. The power of symbols is well known. They catch the eye, are easy to remember, and can be associated with our own experiences.

The following information is my interpretation of the symbols, crystals, and numbers used in the mandalas. This is based on both my personal research and information from my guides.

The Flower of Life ~ This is one of the oldest sacred geometry shapes. It is created around a circle whose center intersects with six smaller circles. Once complete, there are a total of 30 circles and 60 triangles inside the shape. The history and geography of this symbol is quite fascinating; it has been found all around the world, among distant and different countries, without any visible differences in the features of the symbol. Traces of the Flower of Life have been found in ancient Egyptian and Assyrian cultures, in the Forbidden City in China, temples in Japan, the Golden Temple in India, and in churches in Italy.

With the harmony of its shape and the perfection of its regular, repeating pattern, its meanings have been associated with *Everything*—the cosmic spirit, the unity of life, and the many possible realities that nature offers. It represents a connection with all living things in the Universe.

Merkaba ~ This six-sided star enables us to experience expanded awareness, connects us with elevated potentials of consciousness, and restores access to and memory of the infinite possibilities of living through our divine light being. Considered a sacred symbol for centuries, the Merkaba symbol represents the light, spirit, and body of our being. Also known as the Star of David or Star tetrahedron, this symbol consists of two intersecting triangles that rotate in opposite directions, creating an energy field that is commonly referred to as our *light body*. It is our light body that represents the inter-dimensional vehicle of our soul.

Everyone has access to their own personal Merkaba or *vehicle of light*. It is said that once accessed, one's Merkaba can provide powerful protection and transport the individual's consciousness to higher dimensions. Activating the Merkaba within creates harmony with our body, mind and spirit, and connects us to *All That Is* in our Universe.

Circle ~ This recurrent and ancient geometric symbol has come to represent infinity because it has no beginning and no end. It is a symbol associated with the eternal whole of *All That Is*, as well as with the sun, the moon, and planets in our Universe. It represents divine perfection of both the individual and of the whole of humanity, symbolizing enlightenment, soul, holiness, harmony, and heaven.

Square and Rectangle ~ Spiritually, the square represents a sense of being grounded and balanced here in the physical world. It gives us structure in our physical world and provides us with stability. When grounded and stable, there is an opening for raw honesty that comes from our soul; not cruel, not egotistical, but deep true honesty that comes from the core of our beings.

Triangle ~ The triangle is a simple three-sided geometrical shape that symbolizes the triads of: mind-body-spirit, father-mother-child, and past-present-future. It can be pointed up to symbolize masculinity and down to symbolize femininity. In these mandalas, it represents energy, mind-body-spirit, transformation, higher harmony, and trinity connections.

Metatron's Cube ~ This shape is made of 13 spheres with their centers linked by lines that meet to represent all of the five Platonic Solids: the tetrahedron (or pyramid), cube, octahedron, dodecahedron, and icosahedron. It represents creation and both female and male energies working together to create a whole. Its name comes from Archangel Metatron who some believe oversees the flow of energy in this cube and in our Universe.

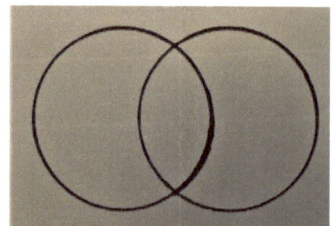

Vesica Pisces ~ This geometrical shape is made up of two intersecting circles. It represents polarity and the relationship of two equal opposites that are connected by their centers. Seen as a symbol of the human eye and as a mirror to the soul, Vesica Pisces represents expansion of awareness.

Hexagon ~ This six-sided shape symbolizes life, harmony, peace and balance.

Spiral ~ Spirals are the connection between heaven and earth. They raise our energy above lower frequencies and help us to connect us up to heaven and down to earth. Spirals represent creativity, growth, and evolution.

Cross ~ The intersection of the two lines is where *"heaven and earth"* meet. Crosses represent faith, spirituality, healing, balance, unity, and hope.

Curve ~ Considered to be a feminine energy, curves are symbols of movement, happiness, pleasure, and generosity.

Heart ~ Our heart is the focus of our physical and spiritual beings. It is where we feel the most emotion, and is a place of compassion and understanding. In a mandala, the heart is a symbol for love and kindness.

Coin ~ A penny from heaven is considered to be left by an angel when it comes across your path – it brings comfort and love. In a mandala, coins symbolize comfort, love, abundance, and riches.

Figure 8 ~ Our time on earth may be finite but the energy of our souls goes on forever. The infinity symbol is used to represent infinity, balance, focus, harmony, peace, and oneness.

Three prongs ~ The three-pronged symbol is not known sacred geometry but has been given meaning from my guides. It represents body-mind-spirit, the holy trinity, the presence of angels and guide activation.

Leaf ~ Leaves depict growth, hope, and renewal. In general, leaves are symbolic of fertility and growth, and represent all the beings in the Universe: the plants, animals, and humans.

Fill line ~ Bridging is formed when creating a connection between one row and the next on a mandala. This helps the flow of the energy of the mandala.

Dot ~ Dots placed between lines are representative of the support of our ancestors and remind us that we are not alone.

Amethyst Crystal~ A self-clearing meditative calming stone, Amethyst works on the emotional, spiritual, and physical planes to provide calm, balance, patience, and peace.

Clear Quartz ~ Clear quartz is very versatile; it can work on any condition. It is a stone of power and amplifies any energy or intention.

Rose Quartz ~ Rose quartz is a stone of the heart, of unconditional love, the energy of compassion and peace, of tenderness and healing, of nourishment, and comfort.

One ~ Beginning and origin, human personality.

Three ~ Vitality, drive, self-knowledge, rest.

Four ~ The four corners of the earth (east, west, north and south) and four seasons (spring, summer, fall, winter).

Five ~ Middle and love.

Eight ~ Order and balance, infinity, rebirth.

The Energy of Colors and Their Meanings

The energy given off by color is one of the most beautiful gifts we have been given in this life; yet colors are also one of the most under-appreciated aspects of moving energy in our physical world.

We are surrounded by colors, but how often do we notice all the different hues? How often do we ponder what we feel when we look at different shades? Colors are a reflection of light, and are reflected in our auras, in the light in our eyes, and in the light of our souls. Any color that can be seen by the human eye projects the corresponding energy to us and that is why certain people are drawn to certain colors.

Each of us is unique, and just as music and art inspires different feelings, different colors may hold different meanings based on our personal experiences. The colors of the mandalas are open to interpretation. Use the meanings below as a *starting point* for your own personal explorations. When gazing at or meditating with a mandala, choose to experience the color and the healing energy that they bring to that moment.

Gold ~ Gold is an optimistic and positive color. It represents knowledge, spirituality, self-confidence, creativity, financial riches, divine perfection, and a deep understanding of ourselves and our soul's journey.

Silver ~ Representing the moon, silver is viewed as a higher frequency color. It is a symbol of spiritual perfection, cycles, rebirth, reincarnation, and intuition.

Copper/Bronze ~ Like gold and silver, copper represents wealth because the metal copper is valuable, but less valuable than gold or silver. Copper is the best conductor of electricity after silver. Copper represents love, passion, friendship, business, career, and negotiations.

Pink/Magenta ~ Pink represents unconditional love, love that requires nothing in return. It is also the color of friendship as it makes us feel accepted and nurtured. It represents softness, tenderness, kindness, and caring.

Indigo ~ Indigo reflects great devotion, wisdom and justice along with fairness and impartiality. This color activates the pineal gland which increases intuition and feelings of being free.

Violet/Purple ~ Purple is the color of royalty and spirituality. It encourages us to look at our deepest thoughts. It is associated with compassion, inspiration, meditation, spiritual expansion, and third eye stimulation.

Blue ~ Blue represents loyalty, peace, serenity, inspiration, and honesty. It is used for relaxation and protection, as it brings tranquility. This color helps us to decompress and remain calm. The color itself is a peacemaker.

Turquoise ~ This blue-green color represents renewal, innovation, humanity, intuitive insights, wisdom, and protection. It is believed by some that turquoise has tranquil energy and is associated with enduring love.

Green ~ Green balances emotions and is a symbol of good health and wealth. It can revitalize and balance energy as well as increase luck. This color is a natural healer, creating balance, harmony, growth, peace, hope, and vitality. It is the color associated with the heart chakra.

Yellow ~ Yellow, the color of sunshine, stimulates the left side of the brain and causes quick thinking and reduces indecisiveness. It is known to boost moods and increase energy. It promotes clarity of thought, strong nerves, vitality, confidence, creativity, joy, and represents the solar plexus chakra.

Orange ~ Orange is associated with creativity and adventure in the outside world. It is also used to draw attention and uplift moods. It is a blend of red and yellow, giving it a lot of energy and warmth. Representing the sacral chakra, orange signifies thoughtfulness, cheerfulness, creative thought, and optimism.

Red ~ Known for representing passion, red can be associated with power, strength, and romance. It signifies passion for life, sexual energy, warmth, energy stimulation, strength, courage, physical activity, creativity, warmth, and security.

Brown ~ The color brown is down to earth and conveys grounded feelings and protection. Brown represents practicality, material success, stability, conservation and care of the earth.

Grey ~ The color grey is half white and half black and is used for neutralizing negative influences, balancing and renewal. It is the energy where all things are possible.

Black ~ The color black exudes authority and sophistication. It is a color of mystery, protection, and deep meditation.

White ~ White represents purity and is a high vibration color. It is associated with simplicity, inspiration, perfection, and peace.

The Seven Basic Chakras in Sacred Geometry

In several of the mandala descriptions, you will see phrases referring to chakras. The word "chakra" means *wheel* or *cycle* and refers to energy points on our bodies. These energy points are thought to resemble spinning spheres that help keep our energy moving smoothly. Energy flows in and out of these energy centers and sometimes they either open up too much or get plugged up and close down. They require clearing, balancing, and aligning for optimum functioning.

Although there are many chakra centers in the body, we will be referring to the basic seven that start at the crown of our head and follow the spine down to the tailbone. Together, the colors they represent create a beautiful rainbow.

The seven we refer to are:

Crown Chakra:
- associated with the color deep purple
- honors spiritual connectedness
- promotes deep relaxation and higher levels of awareness

Third Eye Chakra:
- associated color is deep blue/royal blue
- honors intuition
- connects to our inner guide and helps move unwanted energy in the body

Throat Chakra:
- associated with the color turquoise
- honors communication
- reduces stress and allows for clear self expression

Heart Chakra:
- associated with the color green
- honors the heart
- enhances wellbeing, love, and compassion

Solar Plexus Chakra:
- yellow is associated with this chakra
- honors life force
- port for attracting in all good things in life, reduces aches and pains

Sacral Chakra:
- associated with the color orange
- honors the creative
- keeps us moving towards fulfillment with gratitude

Root Chakra:
- red is the color associated with this chakra
- honors the earth
- energizes and balances, connects us to the earth.

What is a Mandala?

By now, it is clear to you that all mandalas are circular and that the specific shape of a circle is significant.

Circles are everywhere—they are the structures of our human cells, our world, and our Universe. In the ancient Sanskrit language, the word *mandala* means *magical circle* and circles represent wholeness, a cosmic diagram reminding us of our relation to infinity, to the Universe, extending beyond and within our bodies and minds at the same time. They are patterns found in nature and are seen in biology, geology, chemistry, physics and astronomy. On our planet, living things are made of cells and each cell has a nucleus — all displaying circles with centers.

Even the crystals that form ice, rocks, and mountains are made of atoms. Each atom is a mandala.

Mandalas can be seen all around us. They are larger than life. Mandalas represent life as we know it, but they also represent a larger ecosystem and Universe that exceeds the limits of our consciousness.

Mandalas are not something new. They appear in many areas of the world and in many cultures. In ancient pyramids, pre-colonial temples and medieval churches, we can see mandalas on the walls, in architectural design, and reflected in stained-glass windows.

A circle has no beginning and no end, representing the whole of the Universe, and the infinite magic of who you are. Mandalas start from a center origin. This center can be started with any shape. The design extends outward in more concentric layers. This pattern, is known as the basic structure of creation, is reflected from the micro to the macro in the world as we know it and has been used for centuries to emit and attract positive energy.

Each geometric mandala is unique. They are usually viewed as two-dimensional; however, they are often so lively and artfully designed that they seem to show a three-dimensional picture, some even show movement and flow. The image of a mandala always draws the viewer to the center, the center of your being, the center of the Universe, and beyond. Mandalas are widely recognized as a meaningful reflection of both the person using it and the creator being—they are a great source for reflection on one's soul.

A mandala is filled with content such as circles, rectangles, or other shapes. These shapes are adapted to work within the structure of the outer circle and are uniformly multiplied. This creates the unique design of each mandala and brings forth a different message because each shape and color has a its own meaning.

Power Portal mandalas hold a blueprint that is divinely channeled from the Akashic Realm. Their designs provide interesting artwork and bring good energy into any space. Their background colors and design radiate good vibrations and reduce negative energy. After some basic lines are installed to center the design, each mandala is created with a unique organic sacred design. Each time I create a new mandala, every mandala that I have ever previously made or reproduced is given blessings from Mother Mary and from my team of guides. This means that the more mandalas I create and reproduce, the more they are blessed with good energy. This makes the energy of each mandala stronger as they are all part of the whole process.

Using Power Portal Mandalas for Meditation

There are many uses for a mandala. They can be used simply as art to brighten up a space. Some people like to use them as a grid for crystals or other metaphysical tools. Some individuals place them under plants, under their mattress, on the bottom of their water bottles—the list of possibilities goes on and on. Regardless of where they are placed, mandalas will do what they are made to do—align, recalibrate, and balance energy.

The design of the mandala is created to be visually appealing to absorb the conscious mind, block needless mind chatter, and keep both the left and the right brain busy. This allows the person observing the mandala to access a higher consciousness—like a deep meditative state, or a mild hypnosis. The mandala opens a channel for the creative mind to be stimulated and allows the busy mind to take a break. Power Portal mandalas are often used by individuals as a deep form of meditation to gain knowledge from within and from their own guides.

Mandala Meditation:

Meditation is a personal practice in which an individual uses a technique—such as mindfulness, or focusing the mind on a particular object, thought, or activity—to gain attention and awareness of a situation, and to achieve mental clarity and emotional stability. Walking in a park can be meditation, gardening can be meditation, holding a sleeping child can be meditation. These are meditations focused on activity. Meditating with a Power Portal mandala is a meditation focused on an object, on its colors and designs.

Energy can shift just by gazing at a mandala for a few minutes and connecting with it. As we rest our gaze upon a mandala, our mind may become as still as the surface of a pool of water. This doesn't always occur, but focusing on the mandala brings in more good energy.

Stilling the mind is not always easy, some individuals become stressed at the thought and are not sure they are meditating correctly. *There is no right way to meditate!* It does not matter if you are experienced at meditating or not, just breathe and allow the mandalas to recalibrate and uplift your energy. Allow thoughts to come and go and just observe them.

To start, take three deep breaths, then breathe slowly and deeply from the diaphragm while emptying and stilling your mind as much as possible. (Breathing in and out through your nose is best.) Allow thoughts to come and go, simply observe them, and return to focusing on your breath.

Put your gaze on a mandala that appeals to you. Think about what you want to achieve during this meditation and what guidance you seek. Gently gaze at the mandala and relax your eyes so that, initially, the image goes slowly out of focus and sometimes gently spins.

Allow yourself to take in the colors and the intricate design of the mandala, allow your mind to wander. If your mind starts to think about the usual mundane things around you, simply bring your focus and attention back to breathing and to the beauty of the mandala. Let the mandala absorb all your attention, fall into it and gaze into the colors, swim in its patterns. As you begin to fall into the mandala, you will experience a feeling of lightness and intuitive thoughts may arise. Relax, let thoughts and feelings come to you. Float with it. If you begin to feel panic or discomfort, or start to ponder mundane thoughts, just relax, let those thoughts go and refocus your attention back to your breathing and to the mandala.

Meditations do not have to be long to have a lasting effect, any meditation two minutes or longer can change the energy of your day and can contribute to manifesting projects. If you like, journal your experiences to bring attention to where you want to focus your energy and what you want to create on your life path. Once you finish your meditation or journaling, always give thanks for the experience. Gratitude amplifies love and manifestation, as it holds a very high frequency.

The Power Portal mandalas in this series of books are meant to address different aspects of your life, and there are many ways to use this book. You can read it from cover to cover, systematically go through it page by page. You can read a page a day, or cruise through it. You can meditate with each mandala as you feel the need for information from that particular design. You can open the book each day to a different page to inspire you. You can sleep with it under your bed or leave it by your favorite chair. It doesn't matter how you use it, the energy from the artwork will continue to align, balance, and upgrade your energy and the energy around you.

Although I have provided guidelines for meditating with a mandala, it is not *how* you use these mandalas; it is that you *do* use them in a way that is works for *you*. Allow the mandalas to radiate their gentle energy to you. Allow them to bring clarity to your life. Allow them to bring in messages and expand your divine soul.

I wish to express my own gratitude to you for opening this book. It is my sincere wish that everyone that sets eyes on these mandalas is expanded in some capacity. Together with my guides, we ask that this energy slowly infiltrates your being and you come to understand how precious this gift of life is. That you feel the message, the innocence, the divine perfection, the beauty, and the love that you are—and once again that you are expanded by this love.

A WORD OF CAUTION:

Power Portal Mandalas can create feelings of peace and well-being.

Use with joy!

HEALING

All healing from the inside out is possible with this mandala. Green is the color of the heart chakra. It is a color that stimulates health, vitality, and balance. The center of this mandala represents the multiplication of cells where our human form is created. The circles throughout let us know that we are an infinite part of the sacred geometry of all universal life and the leaves reflect our ability to grow and expand.

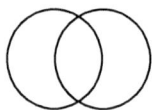

Mandala Moment

This Power Portal mandala allows your body, mind, and spirit to work together in unison with all the powers of the Universe. Use it to raise your frequency above fear, disease, and lack. What would help you grow and expand to your highest frequency in this moment?
Just imagine the possibilities.

EXPANDED POTENTIAL

This six-sided Merkaba softly shines and grows bigger throughout this mandala. The Merkaba enables us to experience expanded awareness and shifts our consciousness to a higher level. The Merkaba shifts the energy outward and, with the assistance of a row of guides, magnifies our highest expanded potential. The colors blue (serenity and peace) and grey (a neutralizing effect) create a space for expanded potential.

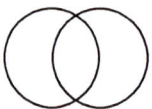

Mandala Moment

This Power Portal mandala is strongly connected to the whole of *All That Is*. No matter what type of situation you are facing, this mandala will lead to growth on all levels. Spending time with this mandala may cause feelings of peace and joy!

ROOT CHAKRA

The root chakra, located at the base of your spine, provides a connection with the earth, the solar system, and all infinite universal energies. This chakra is as it sounds; grounded and rooted to *All That Is*…just like the trees. There is a cross running through the center of the main square symbolizing the spot where heaven and earth meet, where we are grounded and stabilized. The triangles represent body-mind-spirit connections to promote balance. There are four guides on each of the four corners to assist us if we need them, and there are gentle spirals unwinding anything that is not for our highest good. There are eight leaves promoting growth around the outside of this mandala. This mandala is red, a color known to represent passion for life, sexual energy, and energy stimulation

Mandala Moment

This is the space where you establish your basic trust in the Universe and feel supported in life. Meditate with this Power Portal mandala to help you feel supported, safe, and grounded.

SACRAL CHAKRA

The smallest circle in the center is representative of the center of our soul, the base of who we are. Several circles surround it and create a portal for creating what we need and desire in this life. There is support from the ancestors as revealed in the little dots, and spirals to unwind any baggage we don't need. The leaves and circles around the outside remind us to expand throughout the Universe and live in harmony. Orange is the color of creative thinking and optimism.

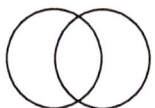

Mandala Moment

The sacral chakra is located around the navel, and houses your center for passion, sexuality, intimacy, money, creativity, and joy. Focus on this Power Portal mandala to establish the flow and balance in all relationships. Keeping this chakra clear allows you to be open to joy, pleasure, abundance, and new experiences in life. Have fun creating more joy in your life by spending a few moments with this mandala!

SOLAR PLEXUS CHAKRA

Yellow is the color of sunshine and of clarity of thought. The triangle in the center of the circle shows our body, mind and spirit connected to the whole of *All That Is.* There are several rows of bridging lines to connect us with everything around us, and multiple layers of leaves for expanding out with grace. There are spirals gently moving things out of our way, while our guides stand by to support us as we journey through life discovering who we are.

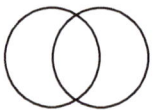

Mandala Moment

The solar plexus chakra located above the navel is where self-confidence is established and where you find peace in who you are in this life. The solar plexus chakra can provide you a view of your ego and of your personality. This is also the area where most of your organs are located…your physical vitality and energy centers. Use this Power Portal mandala to connect to your wisdom, strength, and power. You are vibrant. Be kind and gentle with yourself and with others.

HEART CHAKRA

The best color to balance and bring in good health and wealth is green. The center Merkaba represents our divine being, it is crossed through the middle to represent where heaven and earth meet in our soul. It is then connected to a circle, to the Universe, to infinity. Spirals unwind and guides are ready to go to work to help us to become *love in action*.

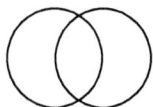

Mandala Moment

The heart chakra is located at heart level in the center of your body. Love, compassion, gratitude and forgiveness of self and others reside at its core. This chakra is about humbly taking care of yourself first and then being of service to others. When you have positive thoughts and actions, you are love in motion. Use the Power Portal mandala to stay in the frequency of love.

THROAT CHAKRA

The throat chakra is located at the base of the neck. It is all about expressing ourselves through sound, thus inspiring and empowering ourselves and others. This mandala has the colors of blue and green, bringing in a harmonious tranquil energy. The circle in the center represents the throat opening, where our own unique sound and frequency come from. This circle is connected to the whole of who we are via several lines. These lines create both squares, triangles and Merkabas, bringing in an honest stability, higher harmony, and a connection to *All That Is*. There are guides to provide support for growth around the infinite circle. There is representation of the Flower of Life in the ring of circles, with bridging lines connecting us to all living things in the Universe.

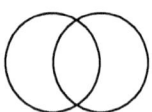

Mandala Moment

Speak, sing, and communicate with dignity and truth. Listen to your own beautiful sounds and the resonance that surrounds you. Use this Power Portal mandala to feel and hear your own unique frequency and to clearly communicate your truth in all possible ways.

THIRD EYE CHAKRA

Intuition, wisdom, and inner guidance are at the core of the third eye chakra located in the middle of the forehead. This mandala represents the human eye. The circle is the pupil of the eye, an infinite line with no beginning and no end. It also reflects holiness of who we are in this moment. There are several spirals to filter out what we do not need to see or feel; as well as a row of very active guides to assist with this process of seeing, feeling, and using our own intuition. Both the physical eyes and the third eye connect to all the surrounding cells as depicted by the circles in the background.

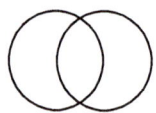

Mandala Moment

This mandala is here to help make decisions with clarity, trust and acknowledge what you hear, see, feel, and sense. Be open to using your own gut feeling or intuition as a form of valuable communication. Use this Power Portal mandala to become aware of who you are and what you desire.

CROWN CHAKRA

The crown chakra is located just above the top of the head. It is our access to higher states of consciousness. This Power Portal mandala helps us see beyond our personal preoccupations and envision the best possible outcomes. Purple has long been a color of royalty and spirituality. It is associated with meditation, spiritual expansion, and inspiration. The center of this mandala represents our own sacred center and is rooted outward into the circle of life symbol, with gentle unwinding and strong guides to assist us on our sacred journey.

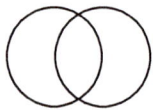

Mandala Moment

In this state of consciousness, you know who you are, and you know your life's purpose. You have a strong connection with yourself. This Power Portal mandala allows your body, mind, and spirit to work together in unison with all the powers of the Universe. Your body, mind and spirit are in balance. You speak to the Universe and it responds to your thoughts. You are at peace with *All That Is*.

HIGHEST POTENTIAL

This multicolored mandala balances all chakras, and the female and male energies. Both female and male energies reside within us all and are not always synced to work together. One triangle points up symbolizing male energy, one triangle points down symbolizing female energy, both interlocking to create a Merkaba. This Merkaba is crossed at the center and connected to the square around it, grounding us and creating balance in our physical world. Spirals, both large and small, eliminate energies that create imbalances in our life.

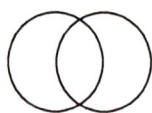

Mandala Moment

This mandala stimulates your best evolutionary processes to surface. It is time to let go and to grow. Feel your body-mind-spirit connect with the Creator…enjoy the bliss.

FEMALE MALE BALANCE

Red and orange are colors of creativity, energy, and warmth—all which support a passion for life. Strands of Vesica Pisces run through the center of this mandala, connecting to an inner knowing. A row of guides and a row of spirals help with gentle unwinding of all that is not for our highest good. The little triangles in the center allow us to access information from the past, present and future. The soft curves in this mandala stimulate pleasure, happiness and generosity.

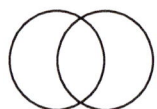

Mandala Moment

Respect, accept and be the magnificence of both the divine feminine and divine masculine, the yin and the yang that resides inside of you and inside our Universe. Be open to the balance of giving (male) and receiving (female) energy as this is where your authentic power lies. This Power Portal mandala allows you to enjoy all that makes you human, and to embrace it from now to infinity.

DNA ENHANCEMENT

Like DNA, strands of Vesica Pisces run through the portal, linking to the core, while expanding and growing peacefully out into the Universe. There are guides in place surrounding humanity to support the life process. The Flower of Life symbol in the background connects our personal growth to the expansion of the Universe. The colors of green and blue create a tranquil, peaceful life filled with growth… creating each moment better than the last.

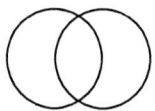

Mandala Moment

This Power Portal mandala supports all your DNA, making you strong to the outside world. This mandala strengthens your body and allows guides to help you right from your inception all the way through your life. Your DNA makes you who you are. What can you do in this moment to honor your "uniqueness" and help create a better world?

ANCESTRAL PAST

Purples and pinks reflect deep devotion, unconditional love and spiritual expansion. The Merkaba at the core of this mandala is connected to three hearts representing both love and the trinity of family: mother, father, and child. It can also mean the trinity of the father, son and holy spirit as both trinities can apply in this instance as both are required to keep the human race evolving. There is a row of guides or angels assisting in peaceful growth out into the Universe in a peaceful manner.

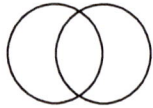

Mandala Moment

It took the love and work of millions of ancestors to provide the opportunity for you to be here right now. There are many things you do not understand about those that have gone before you. If you have questions about your ancestral past, open your mind and connect with the center of this Power Portal mandala. This mandala bridges the love of your ancestors with where you are today. Embrace and honor your heritage.

BACK TO "OM"

The "OM" symbol in this Power Portal mandala represents our center and the center of the Universe. The six-sided Merkaba has left spins in each point, allowing all that we do not need to spin away, resetting us to our own divine pattern. There is a row of active guides surrounding the central core of the mandala, ready to assist us as we grow. All chakra colors and symbols reside within this mandala, aligning the chakras while creating increased life flow and balance.

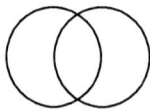

Mandala Moment

This Power Portal mandala takes you back to your origins, to home, to "OM". Are you at peace with who you are? In this moment take a few deep breaths while gazing at this mandala to really feel that peace. If you feel compelled, gently chant a few long "OM"s while focusing on this mandala.

STAND TALL

The circle at the center of this Power Portal mandala is symbolic of an aerial view of our spine; it is an unending circle of strength that supports us through life. There is a row of guides present to help give us the ability to stand tall, and a row of spirals moving energy throughout the spine, clearing the emotional, spiritual, and physical aspects. The Merkaba is connected to the Flower of Life symbol and bridges the flow into the Universe. Pink represents unconditional love, kindness and caring.

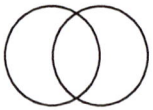

Mandala Moment

This mandala symbolically enables you to stand tall, to be supported, and to stand up for what you know is truth. The more grounded you are and the more gently you speak your truth, the better your energy flow will be.

PINEAL GLAND EXPANSION

The main physical function of the pineal gland is to receive information about the state of the light-dark cycle from the environment and to use this information to regulate our awake-sleep cycle. The pineal gland also continually scans light-dark energies and sends messages to us through intuition and the use of the third eye. In this mandala, there is a strong Merkaba presence at the center. Left spirals surround the Merkaba to clear the energy at the core. They are further held within a hexagon which represents potential for life. The next row is symbolic of a pinecone pattern and of the pineal gland located in our brain. It is accompanied by spirals to unwind unwanted thought patterns we may not even be aware of. Finally, there are two rows of pointed leaves which allow for intuition-driven expansion.

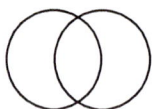

Mandala Moment

Anyone can develop their intuition with practice. Take a minute with this Power Portal mandala for enhancing your intuition, opening your third eye, and stimulating your pineal gland.

YOU ARE AMAZING

The double Merkaba at the center of this mandala has a movement to it and is filled with three tiny triangles representing body, mind, spirit; mother, father, child; and past, present, and future. All these representations work together to bring momentum to our lives. There are two rows of guides, one is always active and helping, the other row is waiting to be asked for support. There are lines for bridging and leaves for growth. The blue brings in a component for honesty, loyalty and peace.

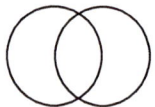

Mandala Moment

This Power Portal mandala amplifies the Merkaba at the center of your soul, telling you to get into the swing of things. Stay strong and have no fear. Regardless of what is happening around you, you will be okay. Ask your guides to build the bridges and allow you to see the growth potential ahead of you. You are amazing.

DEEP WITHIN

Pink reflects softness, tenderness, and unconditional love. This mandala honors the guide within the core of our being represented by the center circle. The circles radiate outwards creating a portal or channel that allows our own divine wisdom to surface. They are filled with more tiny circles creating a ring of Figure 8s, representing that our soul is infinite in its wholeness and presence. There are strong peaceful bridging lines and two rows of leaves for potential growth.

Mandala Moment

Go deep within and really look at your soul journey and at your life. What is working well? What is not working? Where is there joy? What needs to be accepted or changed? Take a deep breath and focus on this Power Portal mandala and know that all wisdom resides deep within your stillness. Have no fear. In this still moment,
seek and ye shall find.

LIFE IS PURE BLISS

In this Power Portal mandala, the blue background reflects truth, wisdom, tranquility, and honor…this is the base of bliss in this life. The spirals for letting go in the center Merkaba connect to the support of guides around the outer points, all who are there to make letting go easier. There are solid lines between the two Merkabas, creating a connection from the inside out.

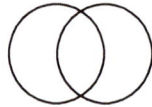

Mandala Moment

Accepting that you chose to come here to live your best life, share your gifts, and be of service to others leads to bliss. This also amplifies your faith that something much bigger than you responds to your needs and that you are never alone. Remember that you are a divine being, ask your guides to assist you in finding pure bliss in this moment.

FEEL IT, HEAL IT, AND LET IT GO

Green is a natural healing color and the color of the heart chakra. Yellow boosts strong nerves and vitality. The Merkaba in the center of this mandala is crossed with healing and hope. There are four hearts intersecting with the Merkaba, symbolizing all types of love. There are spirals in the hearts creating the opportunity to release any deep emotions. There are four guides ready to serve us in this release, as well as curves to symbolize a movement of energy. The leaves symbolize growth.

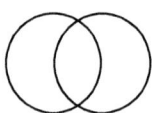

Mandala Moment

In this moment, is there anything you want to feel, heal and let go? While gazing at this mandala, focus on feeling the issue, feel every aspect of it. Ask your guides to help release and heal this energy and allow it to gently leave your whole being now. Don't forget to breathe.

UNWIND, PLAY AND GROW

The soft purples and greens encourage spiritual expansion, revitalization, and inspiration. These layers of Merkabas are filled with spirals to unwind from the inside to the outside. There are many roots and leaves stimulating growth on all levels of being. The significance of three guides strongly reflects the body-mind-spirit connection. The layers of Merkabas are also gently connected to The Flower of Life and to *All That Is*.

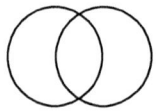

Mandala Moment

This Power Portal mandala represents the human ability to use free will. Use your free will to unwind and let go of heavy energies. Continually strive to play, to dance, and to learn. Place your inhibitions in the center and watch them spin away. Three angels are in the mandala to cheer you on. There is significant room for growth and soul expansion right now. Enjoy this moment.

YOU ARE PERFECT

Purple and turquoise reflect inspiration, renewal, and wisdom. The hexagons in this mandala reflect the potential for life. The spirals help move obstacles out of the way and raise our energy above the lower frequencies in life that do not support us. There are three rows of angels to help us along the way, some are active, and others are waiting for us to ask them for help. There are many bridges in this mandala, showing that we have considerable opportunity for growth and are supported on this journey.

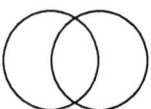

Mandala Moment

This Power Portal mandala brings a strong message: "You are perfect, right here, right now, and You are exactly where you are meant to be." It doesn't mean that there is nothing to work on, but reminds you to be very gentle and compassionate with yourself. Remember there are three levels of guides waiting in this mandala to cheer you on and to acknowledge your perfection. They are here to support the manifestation of your dreams and desires.

INTUITIVE PUSH

The hexagons at the center represent our true potential in this life. The strong Merkaba symbol is being pushed right off the canvas by the spinning of the hexagon symbol in the center. Although very simple, there is extreme strength in this mandala. The colors blue, pink and purple, all help us feel loved, nurtured, and accepted at a deep level.

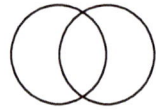

Mandala Moment

This Power Portal mandala is here to give your intuition a push. Remember to let go of fear and trust your senses and your internal voice. Listen to your gut feelings, to your hunches—they are here to help guide you through life. The more you listen and trust your intuition, the stronger it will become.

REJUVENATION

This chakra-colored Power Portal mandala is about unwinding the very core of our internal light, of our Merkaba, and of our own divine energy to allow space for something more aligned with our higher frequencies. The colors align, balance, and restore harmony on all levels. The Merkaba symbol is then softened with the Flower of Life symbol in the background, making this mandala a great meditation tool for bringing peace into this moment.

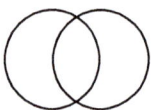

Mandala Moment

This mandala will softly work on your emotional, spiritual, physical, psychological, and psychic levels. Because it works on so many levels, it is a great tool for resolving old, deep patterns as well as gaining insight on things you don't really understand. As you focus your gaze on this mandala, allow your whole being to regenerate, recalibrate and realign. Let the rejuvenation begin!

FORGIVE YOURSELF

Green is one of the predominant colors of nature, and we are part of the natural processes of the earth. The overlapping circle over the center Merkabas reminds us that we are infinite, we have no beginning and no end. This circle is connected to releasing spirals, active guides, and numerous leaves for growing in the outside world.

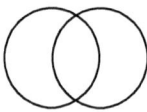

Mandala Moment

There are no mistakes in life, it is a natural process. Every experience is here to provide you with the opportunity to grow and to expand your existence. This Power Portal mandala was created to help you acknowledge your human self, to love yourself, and to avoid becoming a victim in your own life. Forgive, love and appreciate all facets of who you are. Forgive yourself and live this moment with grace.

CELEBRATE YOUR WINS

The hexagon at the core reflects the inner journey, the Merkaba symbolizes the human soul. The spirals raise our frequency above lower frequencies, allowing us to connect to our best life. Layers of guides anchor this sacred journey. Blue is the color of peace.

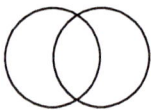

Mandala Moment

This Power Portal mandala is off the charts… actually off the canvas… and wants you to celebrate your "wins". Learn that even the smallest accomplishment makes up part of this life experience. Celebrate the little things and the big things. Be in awe of your journey! Your life is a gift. Focus on the center of this mandala and take a moment to celebrate and be grateful for all that you are.

EXUBERANCE

Yellow is the color of sunshine and increases vitality. Orange represents exuberance, cheering and optimism. Together they celebrate life! The Flower of Life symbol lays the base of connection to all living things and to the great cosmic spirit. There is bridging between the cosmic spirit and our own growth, and multiple guides are ready to celebrate life with us. The spirals align us with what is best attuned to our frequency.

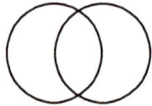

Mandala Moment

This Power Portal mandala is about living life to its fullest with joy and fun. Exuberance is excitement, anticipation, curiosity, knowing, loving, creating—all rolled into one. It is exploring your world with a cheerful and loving attitude to expedite the growth of your soul in this lifetime. With zest and vigor, you learn to enjoy the gift of the present moment.

OUT OF THE BLUE

The Flower of Life is at the core of this mandala. A strong row of spirals and a row of guides help bring our energy back into alignment. There are strong bridging lines throughout the leaves, with a semblance of a tiny peace sign on each point. Blue is the color of peace. It helps us to decompress and to remain calm.

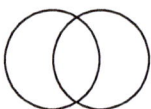

Mandala Moment

Your DNA is a spiral that holds the imprint of your soul. Sometimes out of the blue, things come up for you from these imprints and trigger a memory response. This Power Portal mandala allows you to transpose those out-of-the-blue responses by gazing at the center of the mandala, returning you to a peaceful state with grace and ease.

BLOOM

Bits and pieces of the Flower of Life symbol appear in the center and on multiple levels throughout this mandala, bringing in a strong connection to a divine system that is greater than we know. The mandala has the Flower of Life at the core and is supported by guides, allowing space for us to use our human free will. There are leaves for growth on the inside of the Merkaba flowing through to the outside of the Merkaba. The larger Merkaba creates empty space for soul reflection.

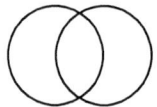

Mandala Moment

This Power Portal mandala is about creating space and expanding your own consciousness. It creates a sense of openness and belonging at the same time. Don't be afraid to be who you are and to be a part of the oneness of *All That Is*. Open up and to use your human free will to navigate through the possibilities that the Universe provides. Bloom where you are planted.

LET IT GO

This mandala is crossed many times at the center, depicting where heaven and earth meet. There are six guides within the circle, helping along the way. Lines of Vesica Pisces, representing our DNA, help us to acknowledge our humanness. The leaves create a stylized Merkaba and let us know that there is always room for growth within our soul. This whole design is supported by two interlocking squares, grounding and balancing us. The spirals on the square tips unwind energies that hold us back.

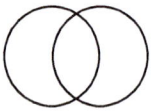

Mandala Moment

This is the perfect opportunity to let go of any baggage that is keeping you from reaching your highest potential. You do not need to know what needs to go—just breathe with the mandala and allow any heaviness to melt away. Remember you are pure divine light.

YOU ARE LOVED

This five-point mandala has hearts throughout, depicting love on multiple levels. Among the hearts are a row of guides to help amplify the love that we are, and spirals to align us to be the love we were meant to be. Leaves around the outside encourage this love to grow outward. The number five means both being in the middle and love. Blue is the color of serenity and peace; grey is the color of neutrality.

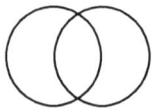

Mandala Moment

This Power Portal mandala is here to remind you that you were created in the likeness of the Creator and…You are Loved. It does not matter who you are or where you have been in this life… *You Are Loved*. Focus on the center of this mandala and let that really sink in… *You Are Loved*.

FLOURISH

This Power Portal mandala has four archangels on each corner, anchored to the four corners of our earth. The lines that connect the archangels cross multiple times throughout the mandala, depicting the intersection between heaven and earth. The layers of hearts and peace signs are reflective of living with love and peace. The colors purple and pink are the colors of unconditional love, of royalty, and of spirituality.

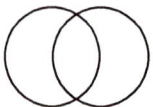

Mandala Moment

Grow beyond where you are comfortable. Love yourself without fear and stretch yourself to accomplish great things. Feel, smell, touch, see and sense the eternal vibrant light that is you. You will be amazed at what you can accomplish.

BOUNDARIES FOR GROWTH

Guides are present at the core of this layered Merkaba. The many triangles represent the body-mind-spirit connection. The Merkaba restores the memory of the infinite possibilities that lie within each of us. The color green balances emotions and supports healing and growth.

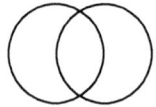

Mandala Moment

Healthy boundaries are necessary for healthy growth. Boundaries help you attract what you do want and repel what you do not want. You are safe to ask this Power Portal mandala for help with establishing your own healthy boundaries. Follow what feels true to your own highest evolution. Stay strong.

ACCEPTANCE

The core of this mandala shows a connection through Vesica Pisces—intersecting parts of circles, a symbol of the human eye, and a mirror to the soul. The core is surrounded by spirals reflecting the "As above, so below" concept. Guides are present to join in at any moment that we invite them. Small peace signs on each outer point send out a peaceful feeling.

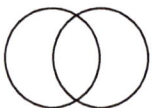

Mandala Moment

Invite your guides in and use this Power Portal mandala to accept what is. You do not have to hang onto to any experience, analyze it, or take it personally. Just observe it. Serenity now. Serenity now.

SEE CLEARLY

The silver and blue colors in this mandala symbolize spiritual perfection, honesty, and intuition; the white symbolizes simplicity and perfection. The multiple Merkabas have an energy-moving spiral in the center circle, and multiple hearts from the inside out on the tips, reminding us that we are love in action from the inside out.

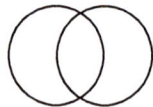

Mandala Moment

If you are looking for answers from deep within, this Power Portal mandala assists by opening the third eye or intuitive center. It gives you a new perspective into seeing with more than just your eyes; it opens you up to seeing with your soul as well. Using the intuition of your third eye, you can learn to see, feel and sense very deeply, all at the same time. This ability does not happen all at once, but as you practice, you learn to trust your spiritual perfection and honour the inner knowing that is there to guide you. Focus a gentle gaze on this mandala, breathe, and listen to what your intuition is saying.

TO INFINITY AND BEYOND

The Merkaba at the center of this mandala is connected to Vesica Pisces symbols, increasing the connection of our soul with both heaven and earth. The row of spirals helps us to grow and evolve with peace, honor, and wisdom. The soft leaf peaks in the final row reflect growth out into the world to *All that Is.*

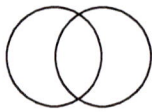

Mandala Moment

This Power Portal mandala reminds you that your internal Merkaba, your light, your soul energy, is infinite. It has no beginning and no end. Your soul energy never dies. In each moment, you are given the chance to use your free will to expand or stagnate with the choices you make. These choices are reflected back to you as you go through this life. Like attracts like, thoughts produce effects, and being your very best in each moment matters. In this moment, how can you reflect the love that you are? What infinite possibilities lie within you?

CENTER SUN

The yellow color in this Power Portal mandala helps strengthen nerves while increasing vitality, confidence, and joy. It is the color of our sun and what we often associate with the color of "light". There are three rows of guides in this mandala, the group on the inside are placed on the four rounded corners of the squares, creating stability. The next layer of guides is surrounded by spirals, opening the path for evolution and growth. The last row is surrounded by bridging and two layers of leaves, allowing for expansion of this revitalized energy, the energy of our center sun.

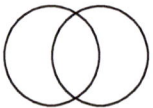

Mandala Moment

This mandala helps to boost your confidence in both yourself and in life. Use it to strengthen your nerves and restore vitality when you feel the need. Use it to add polish and shine to your life. Shine like the center sun that you are.

DIVINE LOVE

It is no surprise that this mandala is blue—the color of peace, tranquility, and inspiration. The four hearts in the center also have elongated Figure 8s through them to depict deep, infinite love at the core. It is surrounded by a ring of ovals simulating a moving atom. These designs are surrounded by large active angels or guides and spirals to raise your frequency. All of this is contained within an octagon to help keep order and balance.

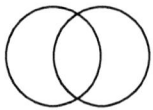

Mandala Moment

There is an unspoken divine love that resides in you. Take a moment and breathe with this mandala. Allow yourself to feel that love. After you make that connection, ask this divine love to connect to all the sources of divine love in your life, in your world, and in the Universe. Feel the joy in your journey.

THRIVE

The circle in the center is symbolic of our soul and is here to remind us that we are infinite in our energy field. There is a row of leaves for constant growth and spirals to raise and align our frequency. Triangles represent the trinity of the body-mind-soul connection, while the squares stimulate stability in our environment. There is considerable open space in this mandala, allowing us to use our free will to create what we dream of. There is a row of strong guides/angels assisting and ready to expand our dreams out into the Universe.
Blue and purple colors bring in a sense of being free, compassionate, and honest.

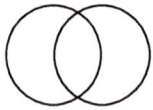

Mandala Moment

This Power Portal mandala reminds you that you are here to Thrive, not merely survive. You are here to bring all of what you uniquely are to the world, and to give your best each and every day. You are so much more than you know. The opportunities are endless when you focus on what is for your highest good and the highest good of all. Open your soul to the flow of the Universe and thrive.

OFF KILTER

The Merkaba at the center is anchored in the four corners of a large square that represents the Universe. Squares in this design support grounding and comfort. A row of guides is present, unwinding all that is not helping us evolve. The two outmost spirals pull everything back into alignment and allow us to regain our highest potential.
The chakra colors help to quickly reestablish balance and feel aligned and whole.

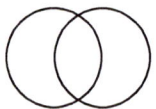

Mandala Moment

Sometimes it is easy to feel off kilter, out of your center, out of balance. Time spent with this mandala enables you to build vitality and get back to being aligned with your goals. Remember you were born to live your best life!

TURN AROUND

Devotion and serenity resonate throughout this mandala in the shades of purple. The gentle Merkaba in the center is created and interwound with the Flower of Life pattern. This reflects our eternal soul connection with everything that resides in our Universe. There are guides actively assisting us to grow, as shown in the outer rim.

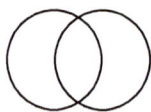

Mandala Moment

If you are not feeling any joy in this journey, this Power Portal mandala is here to help you change direction. You do not have to change directions all at once. This shift can be done in small steps. Start adding one thing to your day that brings you fun or joy… it can be a memory, a flower, a walk, a smell. Keep adding a new joy to your list and soon you will be finding joy in all you do. Live your best life.

ASK FOR HELP

Neutrality is present in the grey tones in this mandala, and there is a pink undertone of unconditional love…a love that requires nothing in return. The yellow undercurrents help create positive thinking and optimism. The Vesica Pisces in the center shows us that this mandala is about the intersection of two connecting energies and anchors to the core of who we are. The spirals align our energy and put things back into balance. There are two rows of leaves, some with bridging to help expand this energy through our life. A dozen active guides in this Power Portal mandala are standing by, waiting for us to ask them to be of help.

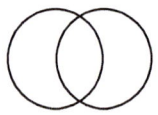

Mandala Moment

Being very independent is actually a trauma response to not being able to trust the system you live in. This response is really based on, "I am the only one who can do this right." This can be hard on your soul. You may wish to find more clarity around this and let go of those old limiting beliefs. It is okay to take initiative and it is okay to ask others for help.

EXPECT GOOD THINGS

The coins throughout this mandala represent silver, not only depicting abundance and riches, but also spiritual perfection. The deep royal blue background represents royalty and brings tranquility into this mandala. The Merkaba at the center tells us that our physical being is connected to the Flower of Life symbol and *All That Is*. Spirals raise and align our energy with good things while bridging us to trust our intuition. This is shown by the pineal gland representation in the outer leaves. Notice the four guides on the outside of the mandala; they represent the four corners of the Universe and help us reach out to bring in the riches into our lives.

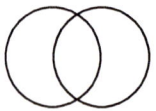

Mandala Moment

"You are a child of the Universe, no less that the trees and the stars, you have a right to be here. And whether or not it is clear to you, no doubt the Universe is unfolding as it should." Use this Power Portal mandala to remember you are worthy. Learn to expect good things. Breathe and let that sink in… *You are worthy, let go of fear, and expect good things.*

BUILD BRIDGES

The muted chakra colors in this mandala softly help bring our being into balance. The circle at the center represents our infinite soul. The Merkaba tips are filled with the infinity symbol, full of Figure 8s. There are strong leaves of growth, filled with peaceful solid bridging to the outside world. This personal growth is guided and protected by a row of angels to help build and sustain the bridges.

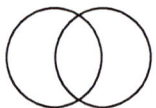

Mandala Moment

Bridges help and support us to cross over rough spots, turbulent water, or other obstacles on our path. You never know when you may need one. The bridges you build with compassion, kindness, and love will last to infinity and are always part of your soul experience.

REACH OUT

In this mandala, the center of our being is represented by the smallest of the Merkabas and is connected to the Flower of Life symbol that is present in this mandala. The angel symbols anchor peace signs from the outside in. There is also representation of Metatron's Cube, the energy of Archangel Metatron known as the Angel of Life. The mandala ends in the hexagon shape, the strongest known shape that represents the potential for life. There are many soft curves around the edge, representing movement and happiness. The purple color is encouraging us to look inside and review our deepest thoughts.

Mandala Moment

This Power Portal mandala is here to remind you that it is okay to reach out. With the help of your guides, you are connected to many other energies of higher frequency. These high frequency energies are there to support you in this life and are waiting for you to ask them for help. Whatever you believe in, whatever your circumstance, know that you are never alone. Do not be afraid to reach out for support. Call on Archangel Metatron if you feel compelled, or simply ask your guides to help you move through this moment.

CHOICE

The soft colors of pink and bronze in this ten-point Power Portal mandala bring in qualities of tenderness and compassion and remind us to remember our beauty, our greatness, and our true capacity. The guides facing both the inner core and the outer world are ready to assist us in making choices that support our highest potential. The five Vesica Pisces in the center circle serve as symbols of the human eye and as a mirror for the soul. Spirals at the center bring in the "As above, so below" to balance the energy. There are three rows of guides in this mandala, one row facing in to help with inner alignment and two rows facing out to help align our energy with the world around us. There is open space throughout the growth points to allow us to use our free will to make good choices.

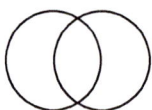

Mandala Moment

With every breath, you have a choice to evolve or stagnate. The choices you make enable you to have the outcomes and experiences you desire. You are a part of a large, beautiful, and complex system that has been put in place for you to learn and to grow from. Loving the sacred being that you are is extremely important and choosing what is best for you in each moment is optimum. Create heaven on earth now. Be kind to yourself, choose high vibes and things that bring you joy!

MOVE ON

The circle center of this mandala represents the center of our beings. The Merkaba depicts the vehicle of our sacred energy, our inner flame. A row of spirals are present to balance out our energies, and align us with being our very best. The outer perimeter has strong leaves for growth beyond this moment. The blues, purples, and pinks bring in the energy of love, self-love, compassion, spirituality, and wisdom.

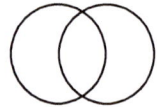

Mandala Moment

This Power Portal mandala reminds us to respect and honor our present feelings, and then to move on with tenderness and caring. Take time in this moment to be in touch with all your senses on a soul level, allow your thoughts to come and go without judgement. Expand this energy and move on with honor, using the wisdom that is in your soul, and knowing your own truth.

INSIDE OUTSIDE

This Power Portal mandala has a Merkaba in the center that is reflective of our inner soul, our inside. There is a row of spirals inside this Merkaba that align with our highest potential. The Merkaba is surrounded by a circle representing our outer world. This circle is surrounded by a second circle with twenty-four inner spokes for neutralizing non-harmonious energies, as well as twenty-four outer lines that broadcast our intentions out into the last circle, the physical earth. All of this is overlayed with three large Merkabas that restore memories of the infinite possibilities of our light being. Yellow strengthens nerves, and enhances vitality, confidence, and joy. Blue brings in peace, tranquility, truth, and wisdom, while the hint of purple provides inspiration to the soul. There is a row of three prongs of guides waiting to assist with growth on all levels from the inside to the outside.

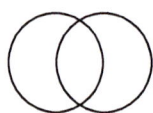

Mandala Moment

Taking what you know on the inside and living your life from this place of knowing is sometimes difficult. To walk the walk and talk the talk is a challenge you will face every day and in every moment. This mandala is to help you live your best life while staying true to who you are on all levels. Breathe and find joy in just being **You**.

WATER

The soft color pallet in this mandala reflects tranquility, wisdom, and renewal: with an undertone of softness, caring, and vitality to soothe the soul. The center represents the DNA spirals of our human bodies and the intersection between our human selves and with *All That Is* in our Universe. Triangles with dots in them appear and are a reminder that our ancestors used water for transformation and for life. Octagon shapes within the mandala show us that there is order and balance throughout waters' life process. There are spirals to align us to the frequency of water. The outer perimeter has a row of guides supporting us and several layers of leaves for growth, clearing water both in ourselves and out into the Universe.

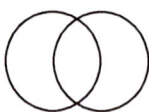

Mandala Moment

All living things need water to survive and to grow. You are mostly made of water and this Power Portal mandala is here to remind you to connect with the vitality it brings to your life. Hydrate your body with good clean water as it is needed to move energy in your body, to sustain life and to help you rejuvenate each day.

CHOOSE & ENJOY THE JOURNEY

There are four strong guides at the very center of this mandala holding things together for us. They are at the base of the four hearts in the background, emanating love from our center to all four corners of the world. The spirals create both an internal unwinding and external unwinding which occur simultaneously in this mandala. There are multiple symbols of growth and potential stemming from the soul center and out to the possibilities for humanity. Blue is the color of peaceful inspiration, silver the color of spiritual perfection, grey the color of neutrality… all which make a perfect blend for this mandala.

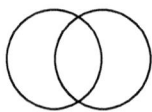

Mandala Moment

The guides at the center of this mandala are watching over and helping you with each choice you make. They are always there for support. Every moment, you get to choose to either enjoy the journey or resist what is happening in your life. Positive thinking, positive action, and choosing joy in each moment makes life a little easier. Don't wait for another day. Now is a time to choose your best thoughts and actions, to live your best life and to enjoy the journey.

RENEWAL/BIRTH

Aqua is the color of renewal, innovation, and intuitive insights; gold is the color of perfection, creativity, and self-confidence. In the center of this Power Portal mandala, there are six triangles representing our sacred energy body. This is surrounded by a circle, representing infinity and the concept that our energy body/spirit has no beginning and no end. There are two large spirit guides connected to the top and bottom of the energy that we are, there are also four spirit guides on the four corners to restore us to our divine perfection. There are four hearts to reflect the love from our ancestral past and spirals to unwind the things that we do not wish to bring forward into this moment. The dots in the rims of the design are representative of past loved ones that are with us to support our journey. The three Merkabas enable us to experience expanded awareness and renew the memory of what our highest potential is.

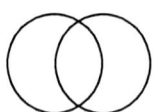

Mandala Moment

This mandala is here to remind you that it took the love of millions to create the unique person you are. Remember that you are sacred and divinely loved, celebrate your birth, and accept your divine life journey. Your timing is impeccable, and you are needed in the world right now.

ANCHORED IN LOVE

Orange offers optimism and cheering, and is the color of the sacral chakra, our creative thinking center. The heart of this mandala is solidly bridged to the six triangles sending love into our energy fields. The octagon reflects order and balance and is filled with infinity Figure 8s. The outer rim has leaves filled with guides and more bridging lines to help us along the way and to know we always have the potential to be anchored in love.

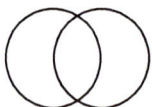

Mandala Moment

With the busy demands of life, it is good to have support to remind you to use your creative thinking, remain optimistic, and stay anchored in love. Be kind to yourself and be the love that you are meant to be. Repeat… ***I am the love that I am, I am love in motion, I am anchored in love, I am abundantly blessed, and I am grateful.***

NORTHERN LIGHTS

This mandala is filled with colors that represent appreciation, joy, peace, and mystery. It has three Merkabas throughout that activate our own internal light and connect it with a larger exterior Merkaba. There are guides facing both the inside and the outside of this mandala and bring support to multiple dimensions. There is a row of hearts facing outward, filled with angels. There are also several small spirals that align our energy with the energy of Nature and with *All That Is*.

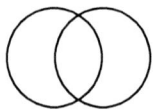

Mandala Moment

This Power Portal mandala represents an energy field where our ancestors and loved ones can be felt, just like the Northern Lights in the sky. Guides from multiple dimensions are working to assist you on all levels. When you reflect with this mandala, claim your divine birthright, the light of your soul, and all the good energy from the love of your ancestors.

LEGIONS OF ANGELS

This hand-drawn mandala starts with a tiny merkaba filled with a spiral that balances and aligns the core of our beings. There are three rows of angels, activating legions of angels who will be ready to assist. *A legion of angels is equal to one hundred and forty-four thousand angels or guides.* There are curvy leaves throughout for pleasurable expansion of the human experience. The outer Merkaba is filled with bridging to connect us from the inside to the outer world. The blue tones bring in a peaceful and tranquil alignment.

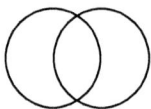

Mandala Moment

This Power Portal mandala is here to remind you that you have literally hundreds of angels assisting you each moment and that there are hundreds more waiting to hear your call. Guides and angels cannot override human free will, that is why it is so important to ask them for help. You don't need to be specific, even asking for guidance and protection throughout each moment will spring them into action. As you gaze at this mandala, ask the legions of angels to gently guide you through your day.

BALANCE AND HARMONY

This Power Portal mandala has a Merkaba in the center, and the center is divided into three triangles symbolizing mind-body-spirit connections. Two rows of active angels are present to help maintain balance while a row of tiny hearts amplify love all around. The Flower of Life symbol brings a connection to *All That Is*. This mandala also features twelve bridged leaf points on the outer rim for expanded growth. All the colors of the chakras are present and help bring us into alignment.

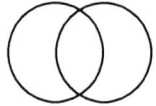

Mandala Moment

This mandala balances and harmonizes the energy and guides you to where you want to be. It enables expanded awareness, connecting you to your true potential. Are you feeling balanced and in harmony with everything around you? Do you think you are aware of your true potential? Meditating with this mandala for as little as two minutes will help strengthen the connection between you and everything around you.

EYE ON THE EARTH

This hand-drawn mandala has an earthy look not only by its design, but also by the colors brown, bronze, and gold. This gives it a down-to-earth, grounded feeling of protection. The flow of the Merkaba from the center out create leaves that flow right to the outside tips. This shows that everything has a flow and is connected on a deeper level than we may know. The spirals help us gain momentum in this life by continually upgrading our energy.

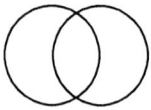

Mandala Moment

This Power Portal mandala was created to let you know that there is no need to worry. You are taken care of. "Whether or not it is clear to you, no doubt the Universe is unfolding as it should. Therefore, be at peace with God, whatever you conceive God to be. Whatever your labors and aspirations, in the noisy confusion of life, keep peace in your soul. With all its sham, drudgery, and broken dreams, it is still a beautiful world. Be cheerful. Strive to be happy."

SPOT ON

The Flower of Life is the sacred geometry symbol that life is based on. We are linked to its energy from conception. Two rows of guides are working with us to activate our intuition and are represented by the pineal gland leaf design. Large spirals on the outside help keep our frequency high and flow gently into the outer leaves, allowing natural unfolding and growth to transpire.

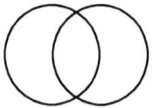

Mandala Moment

This Power Portal mandala shows that from now to infinity, the process of life is unfolding as it should. All experiences—good, bad, and indifferent—have shaped you to be you in this moment. You are perfect, right here, right now. There are guides waiting for you to ask them to help you reach your full potential. Wherever you are today, whatever your situation, know that you are exactly where you are meant to be.

ANGELS AMONG US

Purple is the color of great devotion and wisdom. The swirling row of angels around the core of this mandala are here to remind us that angels are always around. The Flower of Life symbol and the curvy lines throughout represent nurturing and generosity. There are tiny spirals on the outer leaf tips for added expansion.

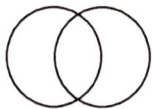

Mandala Moment

Angels come in many forms. They may be a pet, a butterfly, or a friend. They are here to bring us peace, support, and comfort when we need it most. You can ask them to guard, comfort, and help—you, your family, and others in the world. This Power Portal mandala connects you to your angels. Remember to ask them for your heart's desire.

GRATITUDE STARTS WITHIN

The soft chakra colors align and balance us the moment we look at them. The stylized Merkaba at the center is filled with Vesica Pisces symbols to show the common ground between our own soul and the world we live in. The row of active guides help bridge and expand this common ground we share. This common ground is further amplified by leaf points and bridging lines.

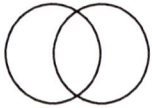

Mandala Moment

Gratitude is a very high vibration and helps keep our vibrations high so that we can manifest the experiences we desire. Allow gratitude to ooze from your soul to every pore of your being and out into all your life experiences. Start and end your day with gratitude. Look at the center of this Power Portal mandala and allow gratitude to flow.

LOVE WHERE YOU LIVE

The solid triangle at the center of this mandala represents connection to higher harmony. It also forms a Merkaba with a second triangle, one that has three tiny hearts on each of its three tips. The number three is about self-knowledge and rest, linked to truly loving ourselves. There is a row of guides for support, and inverted peace signs attached to the outer tips of the leaves. There are bridging lines throughout and together with the full design, help us connect to our Universe. The brown and bronze earthy tones are very grounding and great conductors of energy.

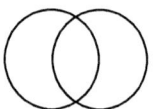

Mandala Moment

The Universe is filled with unlimited abundance for all. Honor the triad of your soul: your body-mind-spirit connection. You are omnipotent, omniscient, and omnipresent as is the land on which you live. All is sacred, strive to harm nothing. Use this Power Portal mandala to discover the possibilities for creating balance, peace, and health with Nature, the Earth, the Universe and beyond.
Love where you live.

PEACEFUL LIFE

Indigo and purple imply peaceful existence in a fair and impartial world. The Vesica Pisces symbols at the center serve as a symbol of the human eye and as a mirror to the soul. They are connected to a row of angels and filled with tiny peace signs. All of this is pointed outward with leaves for growth.

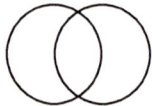

Mandala Moment

To develop a peaceful existence, you must first find peace within your soul. The world as you know it, is a mirror of the energy of all those that live in it. This Power Portal mandala radiates peace wherever it is placed. Focusing your intention on it brings a peaceful pulse to your being and to your life. Peace be with you.

LISTEN TO THE SPIRIT OF THE EARTH

The spirit of the earth Power Portal mandala has an earthy bronze quality. The appearance of guides and free-floating dots represent our sacred orbit, our sacred journey while being supported by masters, teachers, loved ones, angels, and guides. There is a cross line in the center, reflecting the intersection of heaven and earth. Several layers of bridging span out to the edge of the grounding squares on the outer perimeter. Tiny leaves reach out for continual growth.

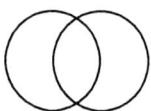

Mandala Moment

You are one with the earth and all that has been created upon it. Multiple levels of guides and ancestors support your journey and are cheering you on. You can continually learn from the natural processes around you. Use your intuition to listen to Mother Nature, listen to the spirit of the earth, and know that you are a part of this magical system.

RAINBOW WARRIOR

The chakra colors revitalize our whole system and create balance. Vesica Pisces are formed in the center of the circle. They represent the space in our soul where everything comes together in perfect unison. There is a strong representation of guides surrounded by Figure 8s, the infinity symbol. Spirals connect us to higher frequencies to assist in making the world a better place. The edging on the leaves creates a solid connection to healing and everything in our Universe. Rainbow Warriors heal in all dimensions, times, and spaces. They know that they are healers. They have a very strong Creator, Earth, and Universe connection. They work with a team of angels, guides, masters, and ancestors to heal all they encounter. They raise the energy by their presence and are here to usher mankind and the earth into a more peaceful and loving existence

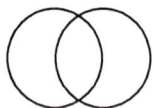

Mandala Moment

By spending time with this Power Portal mandala, you can connect to the Rainbow Warrior that lies within and to the Universal light that leads our way.

Conclusion

Our whole Universe is made up of matter and energy. Matter is anything that has mass and takes up space. Energy is more abstract. In physics, energy has the ability to do work—the ability to move or cause change in matter. In effect, the amount of energy something has or takes refers to its capacity to cause things to happen.

Energy is naturally always conserved—it cannot be created or destroyed. It can, however, be transferred between objects or systems by other interactions or forces. For example, the energy in vegetables is transferred to the people who eat and digest them. This converts into energy for the people who consumed the vegetables so that they can use this energy in another capacity.

We are all connected to each other and to *All That Is* through our energy fields. Taking time to learn to connect with our own individual energy fields and then learn to connect our energy with trees, plants, animals and other human beings is what brings harmony to our lives. Connecting to the divine universal energy is regenerating and very peaceful.

Have you ever wandered into a room and wished you could run away? A place where you just got a bad feeling? It is because you feel and recognize the negative energy? Or have you had the opposite experience? Where you walk into a room and feel so happy that you could stay forever? This good feeling is because the energy is clear, balanced and aligned with your own energy. When you feel this good energy, it is supportive and in harmony with your own energy on many levels.

Feelings surrounding energy happen each and every moment of our lives. Learning how to recalibrate and regenerate our energy can change the outcome of the situation around us. It does not mean that bad things never happen and that things never go wrong, it just means that by understanding our energy we have another tool to help ourselves and those around us cope better with whatever is happening.

How we connect to what we feel and to what is happening around us energetically can cause us to make judgements about ourselves and others, causing additional stress to our lives. You no doubt have heard that it takes only seven seconds to make a first impression? This is because in those seven seconds, we automatically use all our senses to analyze a person, including their energy.

Everything Is Energy—from the chair you are sitting in, the room you are located in, the planet you reside on, the person you sit beside—right down to your beating heart and to your own divine spirit—*Everything is energy*. Your energy should flow free and follow the patterns of nature like the wind and the rivers—soft, bending, shaping and filled with movement and life and joy.

We are each unique and carry our own individual energy frequency. We each have our own unique purpose for bringing this energy to this life.

Each of you is special and *you* are the *only* one that can do what *you* came here to do—to learn and to be.

You are created in the likeness of the creator being, an unlimited being, with unlimited resources.

You were born rich and abundant.

SACRED GEOMETRY FOR THE SOUL

Acknowledgements

Thank you to the creator that runs our amazing interactive Universe. Thank you for always giving me a sign and sending amazing souls into my life. Thank you to my guides and ancestors for their support, love and guidance.

Thank you to the Power Portal Mandalas for choosing me to be the creative human to bring their sacred energy back to our world. I am humbled by these experiences and treasure each sacred moment of this life.

Thank-you Deanna Litz (Owner of *Powerful Nature Coaching & Consulting* - www.powerfulnature.com) for your beautiful light, for being the caring soul that you are, for understanding that this business did not fit in a traditional box, that it morphed and changed along the way many times. Thank you for keeping me focused and always encouraging me to keep going and to reach for my highest potential no matter what else was going on around me. You have been my grounding rod more times than you know.

Thank you Jeanne Martinson (Wood Dragon Books) for coming back into my life with the new role of being my editor and publisher. What a great surprise for me! I am blessed to have worked with you on many levels in this life and call you friend. You have always helped me to expand my horizons with your keen mind and caring heart.

Thank you Jim for your support on so many levels over the last half a century! I cannot begin to list all the things I am grateful to you for! As my partner in life we have shared so much. Love you a heap!

Thank you to my clients and business associates. I continue to learn and grow from our time together. Without your support, this project would not have been be possible. Thank you.

Thank you to my family and friends in this life for their love, support, editing and endless hours of listening to my excitement about mandalas and energy work. You have no idea how I treasure each of you.

ANN CHATFIELD

To those of you who have purchased Sacred Geometry for the Soul or have somehow helped along the way, my deepest appreciation and love. If you sometimes wonder where I am or can't reach me, I am in my home office nicknamed "mandala land" … channeling more mandalas.

About the Author

Ann Chatfield is an intuitive who has spent her life doing energy work on herself and others while searching for modalities that are simple and easy to use. She is a both a Usui and Prana Reiki Master, an Access Bars practitioner, a Yuen Method practitioner, and an Advanced Akashic Record practitioner. While learning and working in these modalities, she continually asked for something easy and simple to use, as most people can not or do not dedicate hours a week to working at improving their own energy.

She has channeled and developed the *Power Portal Mandalas* as an easy way for others to do energy upgrades on themselves in their own time and space. Each volume in this series works in a different way as each set of mandalas carries its own unique message. The mandalas are designed to gently move energy, balance body systems and upgrade the energy of anyone that sees them. They work on the premise that you are not broken. By keeping your own energy field balanced, you have the opportunity to reach your own highest potential in every moment.

As a reader of these books, you can browse through the volumes systematically from cover to cover, intuitively open to a page and focus on the mandala chosen, or deliberately pick a favorite that really helps you move back to your highest potential quickly.

Working with Ann

It is Ann's gift and greatest honor to be able to assist individuals to reach their highest potential by sharing her Power Portal Mandalas, as well as conducting individual sessions, group sessions, and customized sessions for teams, families, and organizations.

Some of the most common issues we delve into during a session:

- Gaining greater clarity about who you are and why you are here
- Having better health
- Bringing more love into your life
- Clearing issues around money
- Increasing abundance flow

- Developing better relationships
- Experiencing your best life
- Gaining productivity and efficiency

If you have a favorite Power Portal Mandala from this book, clothing items featuring the Power Portal Mandalas and digital downloads are available for purchase on the website www.powerportals.com. The Power Portal Mandala called HEALING is always available as a free download at www.powerportal.com.

To book an individual session with Ann or inquire about group or customized sessions, visit www.powerportalsolutions.com or email ann@powerportalsolutions.com.

To see the latest news about Ann and the Sacred Geometry for the Soul book series, see the Facebook page: Power Portal Solutions

www.ingramcontent.com/pod-product-compliance
Lightning Source LLC
Chambersburg PA
CBHW041152230426
43673CB00036B/503